Baby Panda

Story by Beverley Randell
Illustrations by Margaret Power

Mother Panda and Baby Panda

are in the snow.

Oh, no!

Look at Baby Panda!

Mother Panda

is looking for Baby Panda.

Mother Panda

is looking in the trees.

Mother Panda is looking
up the hill.

Where is Baby Panda?

Mother Panda is looking
down the hill.
Where **is** Baby Panda?

Baby Panda

is down here in the snow.

A big cat

can see Baby Panda.

Mother Panda sees Baby Panda
and the big cat.

Mother Panda

runs down the hill.

The big cat

sees Mother Panda coming.

The big cat

runs away.

Baby Panda is safe.